Swimming Through Marble

Gillie Robic

LIVE CANON

First Published in 2016
By Live Canon Ltd
www.livecanon.co.uk

978-1-909703-17-9

Cover Image: NewYork State fossils. Sea scorpions (Jaekelopterus rhenaniae), a species of the extinct arthropod group, Eurypterid.

Edited by Helen Eastman for Live Canon
www.livecanon.co.uk

Swimming Through Marble

GILLIE ROBIC was born in Bombay, a great love and abiding influence on her. As was the custom, she was sent away to school in England, which she found a difficult transition after the colour and richness of India. She attended the Sorbonne and L'U.C.A.D. in Paris, after which she studied Theatre Design at the Central School of Art in London. As part of the drop-out generation, she completed none of these courses. After a lot of travelling and different jobs, she became a puppeteer and voice artist, working in theatre, film and television, and with her own ad hoc company, Suspended Animation. She is a performer, designer, maker, director, teacher and writer. Ten years ago, she turned to poetry. This is her first collection.

Acknowledgments

The following poems have been previously published in the following journals:

'Vault', 'Mumbai Flood', 'Flyover', 'Boulevardière', 'Spring Break', 'Mumbai Acrobat', 'Shelter', 'Peckham Passagiata', 'Rye Lane Calls' in *South Bank Poetry;* 'Master of Gossamer', 'Under the Garden', 'Bridge' in *Lunar Poetry;* 'Breaking the Fast', 'DNA' in *East Coast Literary Review;* 'Remote Control' published by Kind of a Hurricane Press; 'Greenroom' in *Undine Zine;* 'Nightwing' in *Kindred Spirit Magazine*

Contents

I

II

III

IV

For Michel

I

Shifting Time Zones

Once again, gaping boxes unground me,
down me in quicksand, unable to move.
Routines, unhooked from their outlined histories,
flounder in an ocean of bubble and newsprint.
Shells, broken corals, frayed towels and pebbles,
my beach time drifts through an hourglass, salty, unpolished.
Faster clocks wind me up, jangle me to scramble.
Oiled and accurate from the rigour of winter
a colder city beckons with well-tended hands.

A colder city beckons. With well-tended hands
oiled and accurate from the rigour of winter,
faster clocks wind me up, jangle me to scramble
my beach time. Drifts through an hour-glass, salty unpolished
shells, broken corals, frayed towels and pebbles
flounder in an ocean of bubble and newsprint.
Routines, unhooked from their outlined histories,
down me in quicksand, unable to move.
Once again, gaping boxes unground me.

Gin and Samosas

Sundays at the Juhu shack, blind-light striped the interior,
outside the simmer of shells waited to pop underfoot; the tide receded
far, far from my afternoon, revealing thousands of tiny crab-rolled balls.
I longed for the wet ooze of sand to suck between my toes,
for the smell of sea spray instead of gin and samosas,
for the sound of waves to drown the slap of cards, fingernails
on green baize and the rattle of chips. But I was lucky,
a mascot for my ice-clink mother, held captive by her glare
glasses and her elegant cigarette-holder. Her beguiling smile
illuminated the table like an overhead light.

Back in Bombay she would float her goodnight on a cloud of Lanvin,
ready for an evening of glamour and escape. My father in disguise,
the fright of a sudden moustache drawn on his upper lip,
twisting him away from his safe familiar face, the unconvincing
smile of a pirate off to sail wherever pirates sailed.
Monsoon rains thundered from the eves, a lamp exploded
in a shower of sparks through the dark; fireflies in the bedroom
and the bang of beetles; electric storms and spiders. The parapet
beneath the banyan tree, where we tried to race snails and tree frogs
under roots that trailed into the crepitating air;

where everyone gathered with binoculars to watch the refinery on fire,
distant flames blown up to entertain, too far away for heat or fear,
cuddled against my mother, the blaze refracted through her whisky glass;
where kites cruised the sunlit sky and vultures folded
themselves into the palms, drying laundry coloured the rocks below
and choirs of crows beaded everything; where there were always parties:
cocktails, birthdays, dancing. The expectation of pressed organdie,
hair ribbons unreeled in shady emporiums, the balloon man in a corner,
chest bellows creating squeaky forests and knotted zoos,
air-filled bouquets tethered to lights and door fames.

The relief of men squatting against walls, where pavement barbers hooked
small mirrors and plied their trade, plucked nostril-hairs and corns,
sucked them into little deer horns, extracted the bloody proof.
Hawkers twanged their street calls: knife sharpeners, fruit-sellers, toys.
The dog had to be restrained from attacking a hood-spread cobra.
Well-charted islands of rock in the lawn, each one a designated site
of childish rule. Playing grown-up in the hollow bougainvillea bush
with a half-tined cake-fork and a cracked egg in a beat-up bowl.
Unskilled kite-fighting with the driver's son who nonchalantly handled
the decorated spools of glass-covered twine to cut all-comers down.
I tried to build a house in the temple flower tree.

Once Was King

Camera eye squeezes him sweating between the hottest girls and lights
hammering on every pore every slick of hair and flick of lip and brow
baking from sweltered black-leather sessions in the circled adoration

it's a wrap and into the desert breathe silent tumbleweed animates the dark
headlights probe the unseen mile after lunar mile silver his nerves
lullaby him nodding along to no radio on white noise crowd noise

sees a spotlight in the distance normal space for him to be so
closer he pulls over unfolds and shakes himself o famous shake
turns his collar up to post-army hair moves forward into the roar

occupies the conical familiar white-blind light blind punches a little
macho acknowledgement *thank you very much thank you thank you*
looks round for the mic and sees something snaking down from above

reaches to take it all shook up *uh huh huh* he rises up over the crowd
disappears into the dazzle coup de theatre *what a show* the roar increases
spacecraft closes its loading bay and slow exits at first then warps away.

Elvis has left the building.

Back in the desert strip flashing lights through gold and gambled junk-filled nights
probed and polished over-pumped and dribbling with rhinestones sacred sweat
from jet-black hair oils the inside of the wired collar of his superman suit

stretches one hand one-kneed feed the one-armed bandits *he's so cute* matrons
year after eyesore year bloated glasses cartoon cape able only to parody
while lying still wired to an alien gurney somewhere in space.

Spring Break

Butts and boobs revolve spitted
and dripping onto preening beaches ogled
by small planes pulling tumescent ads
for Nite-Life can't wait to get it on the oily breeze.
Rhinestone-pink cells tucked into shell-flesh
overflowing Ocean Drive bars squeezed out
of hot lycra into vodka buzz and fairy tail-light
jams scarlet under winking palms and gaudy sky.
Ultra music thumping crowds winnow the sands
in front of a reflective Atlantic.

Mumbai Acrobat

The boy dwells in a glitzy part of town,
on the pavement,
his few belongings placed
in front of a sari emporium.

Perfumed shoppers drift around
him where head bent
he squats over fine traced
lines on old card, maybe a sum

for schoolwork, judging by his frown
of involvement.
Now he leans from the waist,
scores the pencilled line he's drawn.

This is no toy to pass the time
in mild content.
Holding a thin cane braced
against his toe, he runs a thumb

along, carefully slices down
with clear intent,
the stacked halves neatly spaced
and graded. Quietly he hums,

while ravelling old string, a *filmi* tune,
a sweet lament,
of longing to be graced
with love and fortune, slow to come.

He holds a cut-out figure, nearly done.
With rusted point
he pierces limbs encased
in cardboard motley, monochrome,

then colours in what he has drawn,
joins each segment
and strings the arms, both chased
with intricate designs and hung

between two split bamboos, stretch-sewn
to cleverly invent
an Acrobat, springily laced
to swing and tumble, fly away from home.

Master of Gossamer

O big scary spider in a corner of the step,
why do you cower there behind a weed?
Don't you know how much in awe of you we are?
The way you float from egg to sticky leaf,
swing across the bush, fly from tree to tree,
abseil lightly down the highest walls?
We too want to dance tight-rope across the moon,
drop from an empty sky, weave larders in the air.

Only when you stand defiant in the white expanse
of the bathtub are you vulnerable.
Some of your eyes on the plughole,
some on the tap, but most on the screaming giant
who might transfer you to the window,
from where you could lasso the wind.

Stargate

I was admiring the marble walls,
lamplit or touched with sunlight,
slices of crystalline growth rings
reflecting each other's years.
Then light shifted, cogs meshed,
the walls softened, melted, became
a Stargate in a Special FX movie.
I thought if I approached the surface
I could sink right through
into a liquid dimension.
Not knowing how to swim through marble,
I cracked a joke, turned away,
never tried to cross the Portal.

Transmigration

For months she lay dying,
barely moving or speaking.
Her eyes focussed just below the ceiling
followed a procession of souls
entering from the east,
exiting to the west.
"Are they friendly?" we asked
nervously. She smiled.

One had a non-existential black dog.
One woman stopped for advice
on trimming a lampshade,
colours of silk, fringes, braid.
One man seemed to come and go
at will, would stop and visit,
a tweedy black Guardian Angel.

The day she died
a large spider fell onto her pillow.
Knowing her dislike of these
we dived onto the bed to catch it.
When we sheepishly recovered,
she was gone.

We buried the spider with full family honours,
in the garden, next to the dogs.

Spawn

When knicker-pearls are groomed they murmur, splayed out on the sands
with their seven eyelids closed and all five tentacles erect.
They stay that way until the second sun dips in the sea
and stars begin to show up in the darker bits of sky.

With their seven eyelids closed and all five tentacles erect
and lustrous from their treatment they begin to pump out light
till stars begin to show up in the darker bits of sky.
They gather up the frou-frills of their budding jelly-blooms

and lustrous from their treatment they begin to pump out light,
to show that they are on the air and ready for the grid.
They gather up the frou-frills of their budding jelly-blooms
and start their progress undulating up the clammy beach.

To show that they are on the air and ready for the grid,
they fulgurate the digits of their three translucent limbs
and start their progress undulating up the clammy beach,
towards the gummy ground where ripened knicker-pearls exude.

Under the Garden

She drew back the curtain. The growing green world
reached out towards her and tapped at the glass.
She opened the casement but who was invited?
Breath from beyond or the body within?

Caressing her cheek small green shoots unfurled
tight spirals fresh as new morning grass,
touched on her brow and her lashes, alighted
butterfly-soft on her humming skin.

Sun warmed and loosening tendrils curled
flickering seeking a way to pass
into shadow behind her ear, delighted
the nape of her neck with a shiver of sin.

Wrapped close about her the greenery whirled
her around and about in a deadly volte-face,
tightened about her body excited
an agonised breathing an uncertain grin.

Now under the garden she lies, her hair purled
and plaited with creepers dry fallen and sparse,
among their small bones with her loves reunited,
all cold in the clay, they are kith they are kin.

Shelter

He had watched London burning beneath his wings.
After the war he settled in Peckham
choosing a house for the garden behind it.
He set about the wasteland, ripping out old metal
from the heart of the overgrowth, burning the rubbish
or burying it behind the Anderson shelter that served as shed.

In the evening he would sit on an upturned milk crate
drinking plum brandy and listening to the last blackbirds.
In the morning he would carefully invert the empties
and dig them into the earth to mark paths through the bush,
strewed them with pebbles brought back from the seaside,
bits of broken china, lumps of clinker and old crocks.

Each evening he would clean and oil his tools,
hang them lustrous on the cobwebbed walls of the shed,
walk back through the beds of cabbages and pumpkins
marked out by serried ranks of bottles charting the terrain,
each one a tiny greenhouse, a little Eden, a microcosm
sheltering a wonderland of rare and mutant plants.

As the years pressed on, he loosened his grip.
The wasteland started to reclaim its domain,
smothering everything in goose grass and brambles.
The mulch of fallen leaves gathered around each bed
lured plants over the borders and into the wilderness.
He sat by the back door, listening for blackbirds.

A Survivor from Salonika
(memories my uncle gave me)

My uncle took us to find the site of the old house.
The bay had been filled in, the gate no longer opened on the sea.
We moved back street by street, but it wasn't there,
everything obscured by what came later.

He called to mind the sweeping up of the city's Jews.
He remembered the platform, his brother's look,
letting go his hand, seeing him marched away.
Families accustomed to bathing twice a day
slimed in August heat, tamped in a humidor,
so close-packed even the dead must stand.
Life in the camp so insignificant
eight times he evaded the chambers
for small reasons: the latrines, running an errand,
recognizing an incomer. Others led to the showers.

Afterwards, intact and unfathomably filled with love,
he married a gentle soul, quiet survivor of another hell.
They moved back to the old world. But it wasn't there,
everything obscured by what came before.

The Nazis deported 60,000 Jews from Salonika to concentration and
labour camps, where most of them died

Shells

Some of them are beautiful
these broken shells scattered across the beach,
for a while they gave shelter from the waves
but the occupants have long since died.

Pounded to sand drifted above the waterline
crawled over by sea grape and then machines,
concreted into the walls of homes,
some of which were beautiful.

Their broken shells lie scattered across the beach.
For a while they gave shelter from the waves
but the occupants have long since died.
Some of them were beautiful.

Seaslide

Discover underwater that fish have homes,
that the sun burns even through a liquid sky,
that some fish know the rites and others are shy
and hide from the knowledge in cracks and holes.
Some smile widely at the garb God chose for them
mixing up His paintbox on the day before creation.
Many are so joyful with the sight they swim in shoals
surrounded by themselves and turning as one
to catch the shimmy and pop of their scales.

Watch the clever crows on the evening sands
watching their role-model wind-surfer dude
sidle up a tree trunk with his very own board –
strip of bark in his beak – leap from the tip out
into the perfect gust, transfer bark from beak to claws
and ride the thermals gently down onto the beach
amid the wannabe wind-riders scratching about
in the flotsam for an equivalent way to strut and match
the oh-so-cool Corvus and cock a snoot.

The excise men abroad sit by the wobbling pool.
Horn-rims and ties removed, they splay their flowery thighs,
order the punch-drunk rum, recover their naked eyes.
Exposed, they stare at the day and the sun on their skin so pale
and the ranks of oil-stained bikinis and hope they won't make fools
of themselves as they mount their boards to pose or belly-flop
or misjudge a wave, capsize a Hobie Cat, fall and fail.
They won't drown but their sorrows will and they can't stop
the carnival long enough to rein in their trending profiles.

Guest Book Entry

I must be quick
they're parking on a double-yellow line.
I had a very comfortable stay but
my husband thought the mattress hard
and gave it as the reason why he snored.
I found the pillows insufficient for their task
but thank you for the clever bedside lamps
(so easy to use in the dark)
and the decent-sized wardrobe – with lock.
The kitchen knives were somewhat blunt –
luckily the heavy coffee grinder was efficient,
though eventually it broke. I apologize
for the stain on the attractive bedside rug.
I was grateful for the abundance of clean towels,
some of which I disposed of in a purple plastic bag
provided for non-recyclable rubbish (Thursdays).
I appreciated all the phones
on which I made many calls.
The flat is so convenient for the Doctors at No. 32.
Please ask the non-English-speaking maid
if she removed a pair of green rubber gloves
from the bedroom.

My Gift

I thought I had given you everything
but I still have my uncured skin.
I shall cut and sew it into little purses
each one coloured for your needs.
I will bead them with sea glass,
embroider their silken veins.

The coins you extract will be tacky,
some will be ruby wet
bloodying your fingertips.
The notes will rot and fall apart
leaving your hands tattooed.

Pancake

He whisked her up
and buttered
the griddle with her
sliding and bubbling
and when she sizzled
he flipped her
somersaulting through the air
slapped her back down
where she lay melting
moist and glistening
dribbled with syrup and citrus
nibbled at her lacy edges
roughly rolled her over and
stuffed her into his mouth
licked and sucked her
off his lips and fingers
till there was nothing left
but the washing up

Doodlebug

If I sit empty-headed, pretending to write,
then something will come to me – well, something might
and I'll only hang onto it if it seems right,
or chuck it away if I judge it too trite –

but I'm rather disturbed by a little winged bug,
who's crawling at speed in a glorious hug
with a lump of a creature who cannot be snug,
as the adage informs us it is in a rug.
Ah! See how he stops in a frenzy of quivers
and braces his slender back legs and delivers
a kiss of paralysis, sucks up and shivers
in satisfied joy at the nourishing rivers
of liquified grub in his horrid embrace.
And now he sets off in some terrible race,
running up and down grass at a helluva pace,
only pausing to suck at the food on his face.

Well, I thought if I sat here then something would come
the truth is, those builders make noise and then some
and the roar from the flight path fair makes my ears hum!
A poet could write something – me, I'm struck dumb.

Rye Lane Calls

I wear me g-string slippers down da high road
the-e-y go right down thru me big toe.

Madam put your tongue like this behind your lip
and hold your eyelid so, so I can thread it.

Only one pound full up bowl of chillies
or nice fresh ginger, limes or veggies.

In my country this is how we dress at Eid.
You dress how you like it while you wait.

Three pound I repair your watch you like?
Very nice watch, old style very good make.

Jesus can save you on this very corner!
Don't need to know to tell you how you suffer.

Parietal Eye

A lizard lies along your back.
You can feel its slight weight.

Your eyes swivel through a more brilliant spectrum
as it absorbs your fading body.

Your tongue flickers over the scales and wrinkles
that decorate your gorgeous unfamiliar skin.

A third eye scopes the sky,
decides to bask right here, right now,

in these colours.

II

Mumbai Flood

She gathers her most important papers,
least important trinkets, picture of Mother Mary
from the wall's high precedence,
her own late mother's framed image
floats away, sinks into the slapping waters
that chase her up the stairs barefoot,
to sanctuary with a neighbour from a different faith.

They sit behind the window silently sip tea
from unfamiliar cups, watch new waterscapes
break around trees buildings cars hillocks,
mesmerised by the altered reflections
that shrink and vanish as the flood expands
from creek to lake to sea,
a frill of scum on the stinking heave.

Later when the waters recede she squelches
through the debris in her home, uncertain
where to begin, how to clean repair replace
her life alone, her mother really gone,
drag out the mattresses, dig out the reeking mud
from walls, dented vessels, splintered cupboards.
She wipes her eyes, re-hangs the Virgin on the wall.

Mosquito Wavelength

There were outriders, scouts and lookouts
who gave the game away keening
and skittering in the corners of her eyes.
She could hear them clearly as she fled
although she couldn't interpret a single word,
not one word.
It was like some insect communication,
a thin whine – but doppler shifting,
bull-horning about her
in changing directions.

They punched their data on the backs of her calves,
kept pace with every lurch she took
towards perceived safety.
But in the clinic nobody could understand.
They smiled vaguely, handed her papers
covered in hieroglyphs, mimed signing the air.

Then they put her in a curtained booth where she waited
while the spies hung on the rail, wheezing.
If her concentration flagged they slid off the wall
and crept up behind her, electrostatic.
They hid at her feet when at last a grandee flapped in
shooting cuffs, making immodest sounds.
He peered into her eyes, held her wrists,
tightened something on her arm
which hissed like the spies under the chair.
She couldn't describe to him the dark bubble,
nor the sounds – although she tried to reproduce those,
they were close enough to copy. He left, frowning.

A green flunky pulled aside the flimsy fabric
over her grey cell, gave her a small black bottle
full of optical purple and pointed down a corridor
to the exit.

Outside she found a bus-stop but when the bus came
she couldn't read where it was going
and all the faces pressed to the steamy windows
were mouthing at her in an unfamiliar language.

She backed away into the muttering darkness.
Months passed before she recognized the words.

Sandpipers

Between sun dazzle and the tangle
stranded when a former tide withdrew,
an exodus of little birds reels un-nested
from the seaweed, flying, curling off
down the beach, hits the sand running
just above the overlapping wavelets.
Sandpiper and sea rush towards each other
but millimetre close the birds veer off
and back again, pecking the invisible,
speeding legs a blur against the foam,
a challenge to the ebb and flow.
Such a desperate race not to be caught,
as if they would dissolve
if more than their delicate beaks touch water.

Showers

A guerrilla army occupies the undergrowth,
webbing slung about and convex with lenses,
semaphoring the sun from petal-edge and twig,
stuttering brilliance at the advancing clouds,
pockmarking puddles as they drop to cover
in freefall from flashed-out bird wings.
All quiet on every front until the sun breaks through
and the whole company signals its presence.

This is

an early morning open door

shadows ripple

flickering leaves on a

slow

float

curtain

silent

underwater film silvers

the unfamiliar known.

Birdsong   drowns   the   kitchen

the kettle   pours   out   into   the   sun

a clump of peonies   swims   onto   the sideboard

lemons   flame   fragrant   among   corals

dragonflies   paddle   in   a   china bowl.

Don't turn on the news.

Peckham Passeggiata

Walking down the Lane as the Peckham evening falls,
peering at the merchandise piled high upon the stalls:
babel piles of vegetables and pungent halal meat,
not-quite-frozen fish displays waft richly down the street,
shiny clothes with attitude, appliquéd L.A. nails,
twenty-four hour barbershops, unlock-your-mobile sales.
Glowing caverns cluster here beneath the tracks and trains,
Ali Baba's railway arches, dirt, graffiti, stains.
The lights are on; the angels leave their trees upon the Rye
and join the throng to window-shop and give the goods the eye.
Smiling golden Buddhas in cascades of coloured ferns
sit with plaster Ganesh next to plastic Grecian urns.
Piles of silken prayer rugs flank reproduction art
and from certain angles Christ reveals His holographic heart.

Breaking the Fast

A breeze rustles through the banyan trees,
moving tinsel and marigolds woven with jasmine
and mango leaves that garland the buildings.
Strolling couples share cones of roasted gram.
Small, well-combed boys with brilliant hair
chase little girls in ribbons and organza frills
through the crowds, searching out balloon-sellers,
windmill-wallahs and ingenious toys.

They have waited out the sun, inert and thirsty,
hidden from the heat and concentrating
on the moment, praying to hold off visions
of jalebis sizzling orange from the oil,
spitting betel onto the pavement,
sucking sweet residue from glistening fingers,
until they could gulp down himalayan torrents,
wash away the dust in readiness for evening.

Mumbai's night streets fill with families
purified by fast and thirst, adorned
with fresh flowers and arrayed for festival.
Snack-sellers tempt with every sweetness,
in a hiss of kerosene lamps and flames
beneath big pans of aromatic offerings,
surging louder and softer within each booth
and its puddle of light; well-come hunger.

Further on stretch rainbow displays hooked up
to jerry-rigged electricity, supplied to vendors
of electronic glister. Slack-mouthed teens
in swaggering hybrid logo leisure gear,
with sideways glances covet the shiny goods
and the downcast eyes of pretty daughters.
Songs compete from rival movies, stutter,
shut up, start again. Like the smiling beggars.

A group of men begin a spontaneous dance;
others clap in rhythm, sway together.
Young men holding hands, ogle any passing
female, giggle and blush like schoolgirls.
Old men with walking-sticks and skull-caps
move slowly behind dignified beards,
then settle on benches, adjust their spectacles
and watch the passing perambulations,

occasionally prodding the grinning pi-dogs,
who scratch and sniff and circle each other,
snarl and snap but always hop away, drop
and carry one, to the next shimmering smell –
stop and repeat an endless syncopation.
Rats in the shadows skitter along walls,
disappear into the pissed-in alleyways.
Loudspeakers chant the many names of God.

My Father's Tales

Perched on the bath we'd watch my Father shave
meticulously in the mirror,
shrieking in delighted horror
when Flat Watt the spider
would emerge from behind it and wave
a leg to remind us he was there.

Pa introduced us to Jimmy the Crow
on the verandah balustrade. Every day
at breakfast he would gleam his beady eye
to coax an accidental crumb
or maybe a friendly throw –
he knew we would succumb.

Later, freezing far away at school
in England, dreaming of the lost
warmth of home, the post
would bring a letter from the crow,
giving us – in my father's hand – the full
story of everything we longed to know.

Sometimes Priscilla, Jimmy's cousin
would visit him and write
to us as well, or anyway dictate
her wonderful adventures on the wing,
to Father's careful fountain pen,
as it transcribed her croaking song.

Jack the Sailor stories were the best,
for Jack would find himself in scrapes
from which he'd manage to escape,
however perilous it seemed to be,
by rubbing a Magic Button on his vest,
which led him labyrinthine journeys to be free.

A dungeon might creak open on a secret stair
down through a wall of dripping rock and hiss
of sliding water into the slime of weed and rise
of tide and a leaking boat to row himself out
to a schooner riding on the moonlit glare,
canvas curving to the wind and the captain's shout.

With such stories full of power to enchant,
my Father weaved us into all the worlds he could invent.
He pulled the cloth over our sleepy eyes
and waved us off with Jack to sail the rainbow skies.

Factor Fifteen

I closed the blinds against you,
so bright my eyes watered
from the pain.

Now I lie here naked
in penumbra, cool but not cold,
just able to read the instructions:

Factor Fifteen for sensitive skin.
Apply generously to exposed parts,
re-apply after getting wet or rubbing.

I apply it to my body
which in spite of all precautions
reddens and burns.

Soon you'll reach through the slats,
split the shadow,
stripe my breast.

I should move further from the window.

Cretto Nero
(after a painting by Alberto Burri)

This is a blackened angel
but this angel is not black.
Once upon a time this was a golden angel,
falling – for whatever reason – from grace
into the molten air of hell.

The angel burned and boiled,
smelted gold flowed away
feather by feather. Skin cracked
flesh smoked, seared and parched,
immutable essence flared and faded.

But this angel – being not black but golden –
beat limbs of soot and crumbling bone,
twisted and turned away from torment,
dragged unfamiliar pterodactyl wings
out of the sucking magma's clutch.

Now wracked and crackling on an arc of pain,
this angel shakes out pinions of charred leather.
Each down-sweep is without buoyancy
but fans a quintessential memory,
till every fracture fills with tempered gold.

The Lost Boys

The men smiled whitely and promised riches to such strong young men
whom they would take and feed for their health and strength,
promising payments straight into the weak bellies of their parents.

Not looking back to see the hesitation of their bodies, the sons followed
along the familiar track through the palm groves. Other boys joined them
as they trekked to the beach of the long-tail boats.

The outboard motor roared them racketing beyond the headland
to where a creaking fishing vessel oiled itself around the anchor.
They climbed aboard eagerly, chattering together in excitement

but on the deck their expectations slipped on slicks of blood and brine
and the stench of slimy timbers thick with scale and rot.
They were crammed into cages, padlocked and bewildered,

while the crew prepared for sea. The long-tail boats turned home.
Some boys vomited but most were fisherfolk, used to the ocean swell;
fear filled them and they cried for their deluded parents.

When they were far from land they were released to work their way:
sluice the decks, scrub the hold, drag the nets by hand and winch,
watch the spewed-out silver slap itself to death, rake ice over raw flesh.

They were allowed rest only when no shoal was sighted.
When the crew ate, they threw dollops of rice at the slaves
who furtively ate raw fish they had stowed beneath coiled ropes.

They existed in a vertigo of rope-burn, hunger and pain,
too weak for despair, exhaustion pervasive as the stench,
green lightning on the horizon, bloodshot skies and angry seas.

When all was quiet in the depths of night, too ravenous to sleep,
they slumped among the glitter of fish-scales and stared at the stars,
or hung on the rail, watching for the fiery trails of sea-demons.

If they docked to shift cargo at some small port, or another craft
heaved alongside, the crew would hide the boys, shove them
suffocating and sweating, into the bilges below the scalding engines.

Should numbers fall, another shipment of hopefuls would be brought
to swell the ranks. The lustre faded from their skin too as it stretched
from bone to bone. They took the violence of voice and whip,

moving like ghosts, for death seemed more possible
than life, and so they died,
receding in the boat's small wake.

Petrifying

Cartilage erodes
ball grinds in pocked socket
calcium peppers muscle dehydrates
sinew withers and shortens
cracks and slows
movement clicks and tocs

a lapidary gouges exquisite etchings
ornaments stone
new-formed in the body
bone aches with crystal
paralysed
petrified

Coral Reef

I remember when the sun played in my waving hair,
stroked its light onto my fret-work cliffs.
Fish stippled colour into my folds and hollows,
and nestled in every cleft and orifice.
At night stars tumbled through the waters
and spangled night swimmers emerged to dance
in homage to my beauty.

Now my fragile, grey-green brittleness
no longer swirls and tangos with the supple sea.
Each tide takes a little more of my history,
every surge batters at and tries to break my heart.
I still offer sanctuary to the nervous,
still form a backdrop to the sequin-flip of shoals
on their way to the deeper, greener blue.

The parrot fish are my companions.
They come in diagonal rainbows,
nibble and crunch at my crumbling body.
Aroused, the sun ripples back in, briefly rekindling
a preternatural brilliance. They glance askance
at the luminosity but don't stop
grinding me into the sands of time.

Respiratory Aid

She watches him trapped behind dilated eyes,
air dragged into hollow collar bones,
clamped to a mask's relentless kiss,
hissing soft promises, whispers
through a tube. Breathless air,
guileful, precious as the future.

Sealed behind a high hospital window
she sees summer mothers paddle cautiously
beside their wobble-bottomed toddlers
rocking peefully in a ninety-percent pool.
Two right-shod feet upon a wall declare
today was fun and crush an empty can.

She turns back to a parallel reality
holding the future in her lungs; exhales.

Woolly Tales

I toss and turn till I can take no more
the endless stone-deaf sheep I count among
my useful friends – at least they were before
they lost their tails, just as Bo-Peep had sung.
Those woolly toggles are no longer hung
on woolly backsides and are these still sore?
You dream the silent dreams to which I've clung
and lie beside me fast asleep and snore.

My deaf sheep quail at sharps like those which tore
the cover from my sleepless night and flung
it off into the small hours which then wore
me out with wakefulness, my red eyes stung
to pray that Vulcan wield his axe unslung
to split my head and loose the gods of war –
but you can't hear when loud alarms are rung
and lie beside me fast asleep and snore.

Such lack of gentleness I do deplore.
Just as from Jove's cleft head Minerva sprung
(for gods were meddlesome in days of yore)
to silence all the noise she fell among,
so you who rob my sleep make me give tongue
and lash your ears with my defenceless roar,
while you play variations on a lung
and lie beside me fast asleep and snore.

> *envoi*
> Prince, in the bell jar's silence I'm unstrung,
> a vacuum I and nature both abhor,
> please pop the cork, unstop the rubber bung
> and lie beside me fast asleep and snore.

King Cobra

All is quiet but the singing grass.
I slither out from underneath my stone
and peer about me, ascertain that I am quite alone.

I enter my old daydream of the time of sacredness,
milk and offerings in front of my dwelling strewn
with petals and incense, begging protection,

as when I spread my hood across
the sky to shade Lord Buddha from the sun,
peace curved around the space between.

I have always been special to the gods;
we're all neglected now, though not unknown,
which makes it worse to see what's done

in our names. Tee-shirts, elixirs, dancing girls.
I'm a system for tracking stolen cars, condoms,
missiles, beer, and government committee venom.

Maybe I'm wrong, maybe this kind of kick-ass
respect for my strength is a good way to atone
for not making sacrifice or praying at my shrine.

Still, they should be a little less careless
with my attributes, they're not immune.
If I feel like it, if I sense disrespect, I could kill them.

Yet here I am again in my old daydream of holiness
coiled round the lack of offerings on my sun-warmed throne.
I peer about me, ascertain that I am quite alone.

Torpor

Concentric circles radiated on the surface of the pool
where nobody was swimming in deference to digestion.
Heat skewered the palm trees, pinning down the air.
Conversation flagged, eyes glazed and closed;
post-prandial torpor dripped over the garden.

Bored by the languishing hour, he lit a cigarette
and glass in hand, weaved his way around the edge,
inhaling deeply. He stared through the curious ripples,
down a small stream of bubbles to slowly moving fabric,
arms and open-eyes: a baby lying at the bottom.

He watched for an eternity, thinking nothing, surprised.
Then he dropped his glass, flipped away his cigarette,
dived in, scooped up, pushed off and surged out into the air,
child aloft and handed carefully over the brink into a hubbub
of reaching arms, chafing wrists, smiles at her sudden cries.

Embarrassed, he sploshed out, fishing for his cigarettes.
Cutting through the babel of thanks, tears and hands
clapping at his wet shoulders, he waved the sodden pack:
"For chrissake I need a dry smoke!" and carefully targeting
his rolling glass roared: "Barman, bring me a goddam drink!"

Kidney Donor

I didn't ask if you minded going,
you wouldn't be far away.
But now I think of you cut off,
exiled in an unfamiliar place, bombarded
with hope and poison, working hard.

I touch the body you now protect
and wish my hands could do as much,
could hold you both in the old safety of love.
I bring my lips close to hum a lullaby,
whisper prayers of encouragement,
I try and cover your scary vault with stars
to lighten your unseen chamber.

I sleep in the same bed with you
and your sequestered twin.

Wallpaper

You are wallpapered around your life,
a flattened abstract camouflaging the walls.
Points of attachment tauten the fabric,
stretch a shadow screen, a trampoline,
a fireman's safety net.
You ache to heal, touch, stroke your world,
suck out the venom, spit away the patterns.
But you can't tear through the surface,
rip the seams covering your mouth.
So you tense your fingers, wait
for caterpillars of light to catch your face.

Hairy

Skin can develop hair in response to pain.
Here's how you know this to be true.

To better examine your body
push aside hair from your eyes
with your mother's irritating gesture.

You're hot around the neck, nape swathed in fur,
throat short-haired but longer down the thorax.
Back and belly one shining pelt continuing
between and down the legs.
Seeds rot amongst the coiled curls that line your womb.
You piss blond ringlets, spit clippings.
Long grey threads nearly choke you
as they pass your crew-cut tongue.

You open your fist to find a soft forest
uncurling from the palm
but your fingertips are naked
and the soles of your feet to the earth.

Your body itches with dandruff.
You hurt, you hurt.

III

Privy

At the top of the palace I found a heavy wooden door, which opened easily.
I had to pause in delight to study more closely the fabulous bestiary portrayed
in its carving. Beyond it lay a high chamber where motes of dust stirred lazily
in daylight trapped up near the ceiling, filtered through an unglazed transom.
At the far end a gallery angled away from me into a marble watering room
with alcoves and baths like forest pools. Geckos and spiders frescoed walls inlaid
with myriads of small mirrors and intricate borders of jade and lapis lazuli.

This bathroom was carbuncled on the building, the privy clasped to it like a jewel.
Three steps led up to a throne of rosewood and green jasper. As I took my place
I saw directly beneath me the impasto of jungle canopy exploded by brilliant bloom.
Painted creatures surrounded me to the height of my shoulders. Above them a lattice
opened to the cool, upper air. Unfamiliar birds dipped past me into amber space.
The roof, pierced with semi-precious stones, scattered colours to soothe the cruel
colic, harmonies that could heal the weakest body cramped round an ailing bowel.

Such mysteries were gathered there within the hole.
I shut my eyes and voided all my pain into the bowl.

Venetian Roofscape

Every chimney is a work of art.
The pigeons know this,
cock their heads to study the architecture,
pace the cloisters, settle the galleries,
snuggle into warm terracotta gullies,
cuddle into high forgotten casements
brushed with wild dry secret grasses,
stirring in uneasy dreams of eviction.
They congregate where people call
for them to be culled, netted, killed;
huddle together on the rooftops murmuring
about the consolation of the view.

Quiet Room

High on a rocky bluff between two bays
I keep a room hushed by the boom of waves.
The floor is stone, the walls are white and bare.
Three sides are windowed to the breeze and sight,
sky-scumble, passing wings and errant prayers;
one greets the day the other sets the night.

A cellophane of silence folds around
me, keeps away the voices and the sounds
that shout against a sea they can't out-roar.
The busy lips all monologue on mute,
their Cheshire grins burn out against the glare
and silhouettes are swallowed by the light.

The little key weighs nothing on my neck
and only I can work the hidden lock.

Remote Control

He kept her lust in his pocket,
casually surfing her erotic channels.

So stepping from the shower,
she might feel the pulse,
not dry or dress but press herself against
the steamy glass imagining his hands
trickling down the meltwater of her body.
Or alone in the kitchen, fingers slick with olive oil,
she would sweep aside the garlic skins and herbs,
spread herself on the table to rub in the tangy mix.
Maybe removing her spectacles from tired eyes
she would catch herself solitary in the night window,
hair pegged up and messy:
"Why Miss Jones, you're beautiful!"
she would unclasp her hair, lie unbuttoned on the bed,
hands all over exposed and picture perfect flesh.

One day, driving solo up a hill in third,
expecting his suggestion in the mirror,
she found herself untouched.
Wondering at her slow response
she breasted the summit, shifted gear
and drove forward out of range.

Torn Wrapping

In a holy land I lost my faith.

Sifting through abandoned ruins I found
an old cooking pot and a folded flag.
A water snake rippled the stillness.
The alleys of the Old City were fragrant
with spiced coffee, leather and hashish.

In the desert I learned to share water
without touching lips, drink black tea
through sugar-lumps held in the teeth,
check my bedding for lovers and scorpions.
listen for camels rumbling through my sleep.

Where sun sets the desert hills alight
and spring flowers minutely in the wadis,
I pitched my tent onshore from the reef
and swam among the shoals and corals.
I met my love, my love. I found my love.

In a holy land my faith was torn away
but it was only gift wrapping.

Nightwing

His natural state being an angel
he ranges and quarters the night sky,
peers down from high solitude watching
over people he could never meet.
Up-draughts of burnt fumes
sweep unfelt beneath his wings,
flow past his face his eyes
dry as the wind could suck them.

What would it be like to touch
down on the dirty pavement
weightless, patter to a halt,
a scatter of dust and wrappers,
wings furled, reeling slightly,
feeling for the first time unyielding matter
beneath feet unaccustomed to tread
on anything under heaven?

He considers the idea of enclosing walls,
doors glowing into the unknown,
a walk among light-gilded silhouettes
stalked by elastic shadows bunching
and stretching from lamp-post to moon,
attached like his wings but silent.
They never glide through empty air but fall,
slide, crawl over surfaces he could never touch.

Troubled hearts bump into his space,
wonder why they have fallen before him.

Stricken

[Queen of the coloratura nightmare
swallows sabres toothed
to rip her velvet throat
in panchromatic close-up
reaching for the high F
over bleeding violins]

(applause)

        what's left is   raw
        flesh on a private skeleton
        carrion for the intelligent crows
        dipping curious beaks into her heart

Showerhead

"Hi there! My name is Cindy, how may I help you
on this lovely day?" She glances through plate-glass
at the sunshine. "No prices posted I'm afraid,
but I'd be real happy to guide you;
I just love my job!

"Rain shower?" She tilts her carefully-coiffed head.
"If, like me, you don't wash your hair every day,
you should also consider body jets and a hand shower,
so you can keep your hair dry and clean the shower stall too!"
She smiles radiantly. "This system is top-of-the-range
with multi-settings: rain, storm, hurricane and spiralling tornado.
I hope one day a client will let me try some of this great stuff...
... or I can show you something really to die for."
She flashes her teeth at a child hurtling round the showroom.
"Isn't he the cutest? Love him to death!"

"Look at this finish, *seal voo play*, lalique-style glass
faucets all the way from Paris, France!"
With a square-tipped fingernail she indicates a spotlit exhibit.
"Or this range of basins embedded with sea creatures
swimming realistically through acrylic; so pretty!"
The small boy screams past, slaloming between pedestals
and tubs. "Oh, he's just darling, I could eat him up!"
She tears her eyes from his progress, fingers
the escaping curls bouncing at her ears.
"I love my job, really I do!

"Of course we have budget lines as well,
I myself don't have gorgeous fittings like these,
I just have my lovely Target towels for luxury.
Now this is a great range of bathroom fittings,
I've visited their facility in the Rockies,
just breathtaking. They're a family. To die for.
Let me write you out an estimate." She pulls a shrug
round her shoulders and sits under an icy blast, reaching
for a tissue. "We all have sinus problems in here,
but my job is so fun – I love it!"

She juggles catalogues and taps the keyboard.
"You gotta have a sense of humour, selling plumbing!"
She sees her manager watching from his office door
and laughs gaily as she hands over the print-out.
"You have a great day now, I know I will!"

The sun remains

                        but we are spun away,
we do not choose to turn aside from light.
We trim the lamps to recreate the day
against the dark tautologies of night.

Yet noon sings danger too; the firebird
must blaze to ash beneath a brazen sky
and deepen two dimensions with a third,
for shadows shape what they solidify.

The woody cinnamon is known by smell,
a bitter burning hangs upon the air.
White embers warm the softly-nested shell,
a fledgling struggles from the aromatic myrrh.

Our senses touch what dark denies the eye;
the heat of dying flames, the new-born phoenix cry.

Dolphins

The ocean boils with dolphins and their trails
where they criss-cross beneath us in the sea
but we are here just waiting for the whales.

The dolphins play and leap and flip their tails,
torpedoes chase and shadow us with glee,
the ocean boils with dolphins and their trails.

A thousand dolphins, each one arcs and sails
through air and water flying fast and free
but we are here just waiting for the whales.

I strain my eyes to pierce the distant veils
that surely hide the breaching whales from me.
The ocean boils with dolphins and their trails.

The sight is fabulous, yet it avails
us not. It's quite a sight we must agree
but we are here just waiting for the whales.

So many pods together quickly pales
the miracle we're privileged to see.
The ocean boils with dolphins and their trails
but we are here just waiting for the whales.

Flyover

to

She carries a metal vessel to the open window,
strokes dust from the plant and pours on water,
pauses to observe the busy deepening twilight;
kerosene lanterns below, along the pavement stalls,
street lights above and on her level headlamps
creeping along the flyover. Familiar Mumbai exhaust
around the smells of cooking fires and shit and spices.
She twists her loosened hair into a glossy knot,
petals from her faded garland fall to her shoulders.
She adjusts her *dupatta* and catches a woman's face
turn through a car window towards her and back
to an air-conditioned evening's high-heeled company.

from

Shivering, she asks the Driver to turn off the cold air,
opens the window, guilty that he must suffer the heat.
A rush of strident car horns, cries and sticky velvet
peels off the fine protection of her silken shawl.
She leans her face slowly into the tingling dusk.
Viscous air prickles her with familiar Bombay exhaust;
she breathes in incense, scratching pi-dogs, shit, fumes,
hears temple and bicycle bells; sees a firmament
of people, electronic glitter, kite-twine, onions, toys,
neon and marigold. She peers through windows
at lives ratcheting past: TVs, utensils, plastic bags;
watches a woman wind a string of jasmine into her hair.

Binaca Hip

Once a week of an evening,
around the radiogram,
we'd tune to Ceylon broadcasting
a popular music programme.

In the treetops the crickets carolled
and cooking-fires misted the land –
we hung on the crackling signal,
tight-roping the wavering bands,

sometimes an unsteady bouncing
off to the left or the right,
then a sudden voice clearly announcing
"Binaca Hit Parade Night!"

Not hep to such hits and chart-toppers,
the notion meant nothing to me,
so the 't' of hit soon came a cropper
and wiggled itself to a 'p'.

Binaca, the sponsoring toothpaste,
so cool, its Parade must be Hip,
with post-World-War-Two Yankee bias
and flash of white under the lip,

The Andrews Sisters harmonised,
exclaiming over Them There Eyes.
The Boogie-Woogie Bugle Boy
cried Sugar Bush I love you so!

Bombay night's rich aromatic
cloth woven of moth wings and gold
parted a crack in its fabric,
pressing an ear to the folds.

We avidly leaned to the squawking
not thinking that this might be odd,
while outside the tabla was speaking,
and bhajans raised love songs to God.

Dog Daisies

Three elderly dog daisies in a patch of dusty grass
survive among squashed plastic and cascading, broken glass,
near warped, discarded sleepers, scrapped and scattered all about
and mutilated concrete, metal innards hanging out,
where a supermarket trolley flaunts its last remaining wheel
through torn and battered fishnets made from not-so-stainless steel.
The trains that sometimes pass this way avert their tunnelled gaze
and gather up their suitcases and hurry on their ways.

The embankment struggles upwards through a sickly growth of brambles
where a youth is struggling down, displacing rubble as he scrambles.
He glances idly backwards to make sure that he's alone,
then stops and makes a deal into his trusty mobile phone.
He's pocketing the glint of danger that was in his eye,
and stands and thumbs the edge of it and vaguely wonders why.
So he pulls it out again and flicks it open, feints a pass
and cuts off three dog daisy heads and treads them in the grass.

The Knife-Thrower
(after the Matisse cut-out)

He's poised,
hefts his knife,
whets their appetites,
smells the swell of noise
as they ogle his pretty wife
locked with her arms in flight.

Muscles coil, teeth gleam,
his confidence conquers time;
metal flashes everywhere between
red hand and bruise-blue skin.

Her pulse wrenches at the risk
posed by the cuffs that hold each wrist.
He sees she feels blood burst
imagined at her breath-held waist.
The public weighs his skill her breasts
restricted by a spangled basque.

They flick their tongues and mark her thighs
and lust exhales as the weapon flies.

Dished Up

You bright you shine you teeth mark air kisses
glassed with laughter every course
banter barter crossing legs fingers necklace
unclasped hands on anything if you please

lay back open toed suck in whatever wishes
mouth the room with magma force
chew inner cheeks appearance and finesse
you're strictly lovely strictly lend lease

but you don't reflect in these dirty dishes
smeared with fashionable sauce
you glitter in the crystals slowly deliquesce
trickle down the drain around the grease

Still

You're dwindling
but you're seldom still
rolling and rattling like a pinball
in the cavities of your flat
or taking the still smoking air
racked in the doorway
watching the wildlife
watching you passing

a glass wall slides beside you
effortlessly overtakes
us running behind it
we still hear you talking
but soon it's a whisper
and then becomes gesture
head tilting mouth moving
still   please   moving   still

Departure

She saw her death inside her right eyelid;
a limitless ocean of limpid blue.
At the shoreline stood a lone woman,
her hem trailed and darkened in the shallows.
Hesitantly she moved into the water,
which drenched and dragged away her cloak.
She straightened, plunged and strongly swam away.

The discarded garment floated for a while,
billowing and stretching towards the four directions,
then sank beneath the quiet sea.

Vault

Boats float on scoops of vanilla and pistachio,
smears on the mouth of an elemental whore
who sucks and smacks the jetties and watergates,
flashes at boatmen, shimmies for tourists,
licks at the blowsy gondolas' prows,
wriggles her toes on the marble steps,

exhales.

*

The lagoon shifts, blurs, conjures
a veil from her ripples and wipes out the view.

The well-thumbed waterfronts sleight-of-hand vanish,
the city stifles a laugh and grins,
gleeful palaces paddle their feet.

Couples move closer, intertwine fingers,
taste another, misted on their lips,
strain their ears for the compass-lap of water,
hear their hearts stumble, otherwise silence.

*

The fog rises through cloister and gallery,
breaks silently round a high archipelago
of domes and towers and wind-salted grasses
pearled on the hem of a spiralling firmament.

Punching up through the white surface
golden angels vault towards heaven.

Cormorants

A thin moon holds up thinner wire
silvering the inner circle
more eclipsed than new.
Boats move through the night
trailing fine gold embroidery.
Puddled quietly on the surface
molten reflections flow apart
and together like broken mercury.
Beyond the pools of light
cormorants are fishing.

Swimmer

I felt you leaving.
You touched me as you passed,
a whiteness in the doorway
headed for the stars.

And I could hear them humming
with the buzz of souls
arriving, comparing notes
of their journeys,

the doorways they had crossed
full of deep red sorrow
and the pain of seeing right through
the masks of mourning.

But here on this star
they were all playing.

IV

Breakwater

Old Beek went down to the sea below
and stood on the crumbling shells
and the sky beat down with a soft pink glow
and he pointed his finger and said *you know
if you watch the wavelets the ships will show
themselves on the corkscrew swells.*

So they watched the water and saw the sun
pass under the harbour walls
and the ships bobbed up and their sails bobbed down
and everyone watched from the tumbling town
waiting to recognize some of their own
swing round the floating bells.

They all came home and docked their craft
and climbed ashore with a smile
but Beek still pointed and never laughed
just stood there muttering *don't be daft
there's bodies adrift on a makeshift raft
far out on a nautical mile.*

The townsfolk gasped and ran for the boats
and pushed them into the bay
they struggled into their caps and coats
turned the capstans and threw the ropes
sailed past the dangerous days of hope
and all of them vanished away.

Old Beek stood silently in the night
among all the empty souls
and they watched for the comfort of one small light
to break the darkness and prick the sight
but the sea was hissing with fish in flight
from the sucking of black black holes.

Bridge

Rat-running past Euston one open-windowed night,
I slowed to let a young man cross my path:
tall and graceful, a shadowed, slightly feral face,
clad all in black from broad-brimmed hat to shoes,
a cape around his shoulders, eyes like fireflies in a cage.
He ran with an empty luggage trolley, too late for any train.

I drove south to the river and turned across the bridge;
the echoing sweep of the Thames, broken lights on water
gulping and bubbling past buildings with veiled eyes
and high architraves, aloof but listening.
The sounds of London stepped out of their usual dimension,
tipped delicately forward and called across the clicking air.

And here he was once more running across my path,
the black-clad figure, firefly eyes and feral flash of teeth,
still pushing an improbable, empty trolley.
He tipped his hat and loped away. I watched him go
and wondered how he was here before me,
how he straddled the river, why we might meet again.

Twilight Shuffle

Slow clouds of indigo and coppered gold
steal light away from summer's evening sky.
The beetle cracks his back, his wings unfold
and blur past treetops humming as they fly.

Snails figurehead each shadowed silver trail,
moths dust the print of darkness, seeking light,
small bats curve shallow spirals, rise and sail
into the echo chamber of the night.

A hunting cat moves softly through the dark,
a frog blinks, petals fall and all sounds cease;
then quiet water splashes, foxes bark.
The overgrowth seems settled and at peace.

The moving leaves are stilled – but underneath
the night shift works with tiny claws and teeth.

Tunnel

I amble through a summer afternoon, almost hear
a faint barking muffled by the mulch of decaying leaves,
quiet crackle under the near-silence of tender stems
pushed aside into the still, wood-dove air.

The forgotten railway track poses carelessly
as a honeysuckle walk through woodland,
wildflowered and dappled in the requisite fashion
for an afternoon's slightly sweaty walk, airless.

A clearing: once upon a time this was a station.
Concrete slides out of earth onto broken platforms,
cracks spiderweb over abandoned structures. Sleepers
lie untied and lichened. Bees mine the embankment.

Furious barking crashes into the foreground and jangles
behind it where a mastiff rattles his metal chain
rings along a tensioned wire running to its limit,
pulled up snarling just short of where he wants to be.

Muscles, nose quiver, teeth gleam, tongue dry.
Nowhere to go, no way to trail, saliva sticky for liquid.
There's a battered bowl overturned and out of reach.
I have water and pour it in, push the bowl closer, retire.

Dog dances slightly, licks his lips, whines, sits, stands,
barks again, then approaches whimpering and laps,
looking up, ears down, growling, slopping water
too quickly finished. I cautiously come forward, refill.

Pebble by pebble a cairn of trust grows between us. I sit,
stroke dog through nervous panting, starting, leaning.
Evening settles the blackbirds and their final comments,
nightfall coaxes out bats and beetles and unseen hunters.

Sparks break up the night; screaming out of the tunnel
a train clatters past us past us past us splattering light
across the pristine station, waved green flame, whistle.
Dog licks me, shackles break, my heart... bounds away.

I amble through a summer afternoon, kicking clinker,
wonder where the trains headed from this empty shell,
wish I had a dog to walk beside. I chuck pebbles,
slash at a curtain of foliage, and look – here is a tunnel.

Bombay Banyan

From where I dangled my feet in the heat shimmer,
the cliff fell away into a haze over the city's skin,
a seersucker of raised domes and temple *sikharas*,
the buildings exploded by flame trees and foliage.

The view was framed by a banyan, roots growing
down into the golden air, and creaking palm leaves,
where the hooded eyes of vultures peered through
air speckled with fast birds and paper kites.

On the rocks below, *dhobis* thwacked a syncopation
with washing that later would be stretched to dry
in a basking, sun-broiled motley. A cacophony
grappled its way up to us: dogs, crows, cries, chants,

the brain-fever bird's rising scale, the shush-shush
of whisk-brooms forever unsettling the dust.
A midden of smells singed the air: sewage, spices,
jasmine and sandalwood, cooking fires and cow dung.

At *Divali*, oil lamps outlined every contour of the city.
Fireworks fountained and fizzed above the street lights,
a hoard of jewels poured at our feet, greater splendour
than any Queen Empress could unclasp and carry off.

And then I was torn off and sent to England
to be taught how to be a young lady.
Did you live in a mud hut? they asked.

Broken Pixels

Sometime in the future
deleted snaps of our lives,
seconds, blurred and badly framed,
will be discovered in cyber-space
by large-eyed, gill-nosed,
descendants of homo sapiens.

Specialists will pore over the pixels,
inventing ways of re-stitching
the images from an unknown past,
recreating a picture of their ancestors'
forgotten tastes and mores,
re-interpreting their rituals and behaviours:

a couple sucking out each other's souls;
a man setting fire to a woman's tongue;
you holding me with infinite love.

Miami Wood

Two guys jogged up the beach
whooping "It's Girls' Night!
We're gonna do it on the dashboard,
a real wooden dashboard!"

She's jammed up against it,
Bakelite knobs jab her back.
She grasps the polished walnut.
"Aw honey, why don't you
have a smooth vinyl trim
I could slide over easy?"

She arches her back away,
braces a hand against the roof,
unbends her sticky knees.
A shiny stiletto rips the upholstery.

Will

I want to be a Matisse odalisque for you,
lie back against a velvet bolster,
arm behind my head, my parted knees
draped in lustrous pantaloons
the colour of nipples.

I want a flimsy covering on my breasts
that hides nothing from your gaze.
I will play the cushion tassels with my toes
and listen to the soft clink of bangles
sliding round my ankles.

There will be flowers and figured wallpaper,
exotic rugs and glinting samovars.
It will be hot and shadowy with curtains drawn.
Sweating slightly I will remove my blouse
and lie half naked, posed.

Hair will cling to my dampened skin
and lulled by the sound of brush on canvas
I will pretend to doze, fully aware of my profile
and the artful abandon of my body.
And you shall come, if I have my will.

La Normande

She worked through the occupied, coldest of winters,
trekked through the snow to her shivering pupils,
who each brought one log for the fire and a pencil
and wrote up the lessons with mittens and splinters.

They billeted soldiers all over her home,
requisitioned the larder, admired her hair.
Her son stole their cabbages back from the cellar.
She learned how to butcher her rabbits and skin them.

In summer, against banks of ragwort and foxglove,
they sheltered from bombs in deep shadowy pathways
suddenly blown apart. Shaken and half-dazed
she watched her skirt soaking up some body's blood.

When peace came she walked with her husband through wreckage
of woodland and meadows, which left them both troubled.
The forests were flinders, the villages rubble,
the earth lay exposed, deeply wounded and ravaged.

He went back to sea and she followed his journeys,
on hand-coloured maps which he sent in his letters
and postcards propped up amongst mantelpiece clutter,
small windows between the dried-flower bouquets.

When he died she kept walking with him in her head
round the limits of long unremarkable days.
Until her legs faltered, refusing the by-ways,
confined her to house, to her room, to her bed.

Her quotidian courage still clings in the cupboards
with memories carefully labelled and guarded,
all layered in tissue and never discarded:
a young couple fades into sepia woods.

Boulevardière

She is so nearly merely flamboyant,
the effect betrayed and whittled away
by knuckles misshapen and freckled with age,
torn stockings mocking purple exposed veins,
unmatched trinkets in a thatch of orange hair.

Layers of aborted colours drip like afterbirth
below her visceral skirts. She flirts with a waiter
at the local bar, vocal, raucous and breathing hard,
until the piquant drama of her aroma sends him
back inside, busy with brandy, handy with trays.

She crosses the street, dosses in a doorway,
magics a tragic fag from her garments,
lights it in a holder, shoulder against the jamb,
surveys her world, mascara smeared in cedillas
under the imperious Cees of her half-closed eyes.

In Parenthesis

Don't bracket parts of her history *(born 1972)*, memorialise her schools and addresses, or catalogue her loves and failures *(married 1993, divorced 1996, remarried 2001)*, nor list her successes and titles in parentheses, like efficient little précis of her life. It's the swathes outside the brackets, the secrets and affairs, the private griefs, agonised puzzlings, unthinkable choices and epiphanies, that made possible those bullet-points of her existence and finally killed her *(murdered 2019)*.

Halo

This watchful city has petrified guardians
perched above us on rooftops and windows.
Their motionless robes billow about them,
moved by reflections of light over water,
their pinions forever strain to the sky.

I blunder about through saint-framed spaces,
seeking a kind of sentimental moth-wing
that flutters against my spiritual lamp-glass,
burns up and falls in ashes to the ground
dragging my vision to the tilting floor.

Vertigo kicks me to a new dimension.
I kneel on stone and touch its bloodshot skin.
Bruised and broken veins ooze with crystal,
shrapnel scribbles over spark-flecked surface.
Colours frozen from a molten core

explode and spin into great mosaic circles
above the heads of subterranean angels
who move within the incandescent earth.
I cling at a tangent to this unfamiliar planet,
balanced on a halo above a marble sky.

On The Thighs Of Virgins

Curved into a question by his electric bed,
he lifts translucent hands and shifts his head,
expectant, disappointed; still here.

The mattress flattened, image more serene,
the box of miracles winks, invites him in:
come, come once more to Lethe. There,

waning and fading but rocking, he rolls
on the thighs of virgins, cigar smoke coils
in a halo of fragrance floating up where

all the green leaves stretch through the window,
to stroke the concaving, convexing torso,
rumbling about the complicated air.

Votive profile, waxen, roaring
into the impartial afternoon, daring
it to let him go   go   gone.
Three silences trip over his poking tongue.

The afternoon you died

I walked into dimensions of light
horizontal slices of transparency
each one deep and clear
filled with your invisibility.
Present
in every curve and angle, hum
broken heartbeat cough.
Absent
from corners of churchyards
conversation, dog-ends in ashtrays
fingertips and laughter.

Were you falling through the dimensions
clinging bareback to a final rattling breath?
An opacity sliding across the eyeball
a shimmer of something
distorting
the petri-dish air, dusting the rear window
of a double-decker bus,
re-forming
beyond a membrane sealing the unknowable.
A drumskin retuning
tightening.

Sacred Conversation

I wanted to describe Bellini's altarpiece,
the delicacy and depth of sentiment portrayed.
I wanted to use words to show how the Mother glows,
the numinous stillness of her understanding.
I wanted to share the Baby's hands, the Angel's lute,
the longing and love on the faces of the companions.
I would have tried to explain what the sun does
when it shines through a high window onto the painting
and how it moves around curves that do not exist,
touching highlights and shadows as if creating them.
It sings from within its own dimension;
my words would be the dry hot air around a fire.

My Dip in the Rift Valley
(after Les Murray)

From hitching through the desert I ran
helter-skelter and threw myself in,
head first, eyes and mouth open
to the Dead Sea.

As if from a whale's blow-hole I shot
out of the brine's corrosive weight,
filled with the awful burn and bite
of the Dead Sea.

Others bobbed high on a shallow draught,
sucked at oranges salted with sea-drift,
riffled newspapers against dry bellies rafted
on the Dead Sea,

back when there was nothing too old to forget
and Jaffa's finest cost a scattering of agorot.

Escape

She watched the ember arc from mouth to thigh
following him through the darkness.
She scanned the moonless sky.
Sand weighted down her dress,
jags of coral scratched her feet.
Sea thorns caught at her skirt.

"Danger! Barbed wire! Minefield!"
She showed him her snagged hem
but he tore it away. "Do as you're told,
go back!" A rumbling ahead of them.
Two camels rose and lumbered away.
She followed, keeping him in view.

Behind them footprints chased their feet.
He tried to outrun them, zig-zagged
across the sand, dug himself into it.
She coaxed him out, cradled his head.
She tried to hum, make her voice tender.
Holding his hand on her shoulder

she led him to the shoreline. The earth
stirred, unsettled by the darkness on her back,
but the lap of waves calmed them both.
She breathed more easily, undid her pack.
They both drank, she watched his mouth.
"Keep the water to the right, head north."

An empty road made it easier to walk;
warm tarmac under a dusting of sand
and a perceived direction, which they took.
Then earth growled, stars rained over the land.
A drone of engines traced by stuttered fire,
sound thwumped across the gulf of air.

Bouquets of flame flickered along the hills.
Fear transformed the gently rising dunes
with shadows and echoes of the thump of shells.
The night collapsed around her dreams.
She struggled to hold him, to hold the future back
but her skull unfurled and streamed into the dark.

DNA

You thought you were alone
hawking behind the summer leaves
but I could see you slipping
gold and crimson rings
from panatellas flickering into grass
scattering your dregs and dog-ends
glittering the bushes with your piss.
It used to drive me mad
but now I'm glad your noisy DNA
was everywhere before
your quiet ashes
came to earth.

Swoop

Wingbeats fill the air you cannot breathe.
Darts of blood and blossom thud out of the sky
but no pierced heart incarnadines these blooms.
Who cares what colour the roses
or why the earth is red?
The lovely petals lie so soft and deep
only the withered edges blush and stir
to catch light on their glycerine tears.
She cannot see you from within the hooked thicket
but smells the crackling of your bones.
You cannot see her hung within the thorns
perfectly filling the perfect space
hollowed for the process of her dying.
No room for penance nor dreams of flying.

Starlight

Paint stars on the inside of my coffin.
Let it be lightly woven
to welcome the evening breeze.
Lay me in feathers and memories
strewn with petals and rosemary
but do not burn or bury me.
Carry me on a moonless night
to an ocean brimming with starlight,
leave a window above my face
opening onto the vault of space.
Walk with me through the shallows
where little fish shall bind me in rainbows.
Float me to the reef wall
and let me fall
through peaceful shoals of manta rays
into the sway of darkness.